Latter-day
HEROES

CHAD S. HAWKINS

DESERET
BOOK

SALT LAKE CITY, UTAH

To my wife

For her unwavering support

And to my children

Who always visit and draw with me at my art studio

Library of Congress Cataloging-in-Publication Data

Hawkins, Chad S., 1971–
    Latter-day heroes / Chad Hawkins.
        p.   cm.
    ISBN 1-57008-992-2 (alk. paper)
    1. Mormons—Biography.   I. Title.

BX8693.H38 2003
289.3'092'2—dc21
                                       2003006740

Printed in Korea
USAsia Press
                                    87899-7107

10 9 8 7 6 5 4 3 2 1

CONTENTS

Introduction 1

1. Philo T. Farnsworth 2

2. Kacey McCallister 4

3. Dale Murphy 6

4. Don Lind 8

5. Liriel Domiciano 10

6. Cody Hancock 12

7. Gail S. Halvorsen 14

8. Liz Shropshire 18

9. Peter Vidmar 20

10. Ariel Bybee 22

11. Steve Andersen 24

12. Stephen R. Covey 26

13. Gifford Nielsen 28

14. Serving after 9/11 30

INTRODUCTION

This project has broken new ground for me on many levels. For fifteen years, I have been visiting, drawing, painting, and researching temples. For this reason, some people may be surprised to see my rendition of a champion bull rider or a space shuttle launch. But I eagerly pursued this worthy project to share the message that we can succeed at something new or difficult if we put forth earnest effort.

Regardless of our aspirations, the pathway to success is the same: effort, persistence, patience, faith, and prayer. And while on this pathway, we need not compromise personal integrity or gospel standards.

The gospel teaches us that the purpose of mortality is to learn, develop, and gain experience—both physical and spiritual. Much of this learning occurs as we choose how to handle life's trials and tribulations. Many stories in this book illustrate how trials often become stepping-stones to greater opportunities on the pathway to success.

The title *Latter-day Heroes* does not imply that those featured herein consider themselves to be heroes. To the contrary, as I interviewed them (all except Philo T. Farnsworth, whose story came from books on his life; and Liriel Domiciano, whose story was provided by publicist Jeanette N. Oaks), they demonstrated sincere humility and deep appreciation for their blessings. Their reason for sharing their testimony and life experiences is to encourage the living of a gospel-centered life. They also wish to demonstrate that worthy goals can be achieved through hard work, determination, and reliance on Heavenly Father.

Olympic champion Peter Vidmar wrote, "The positive experiences of others not only show us what's possible, but by looking at their performances we can also understand what's necessary to get where they went. Whether we want to pay the price they paid is our own decision. But at the very least we have evidence of what has been done, and more importantly, what *can be done*" (*Risk, Originality, and Virtuosity* [Washington, D.C.: Leading Authorities Press, 2002], xvii).

MAY THE YOUTH WHO READ THIS

BOOK BE INSPIRED TO RAISE THE BAR OF

ACCOMPLISHMENT IN THEIR OWN LIVES.

Chad Hawkins

PHILO T. FARNSWORTH

PHILO T. FARNSWORTH joined people around the world in watching their television sets on July 20, 1969, as the first astronauts landed on the moon. "This has made it all worthwhile," he told his wife, Pem, as the lunar scene unfolded. Although Philo, then sixty-two, was not connected with the Apollo moon landing, he felt the satisfaction of knowing that millions of people could witness the event. After all, nearly fifty years earlier when he was only fourteen, Philo had envisioned the fundamentals of television.

Philo was born in a log cabin near Beaver, Utah. His father was a farmer who frequently moved his family in search of better farmland. As a curious young farm boy, Philo liked to experiment with electrical devices, including the gramophone and the hand-cranked telephone. His love for science and his lofty imagination led him to become an inventor.

While living on a ranch near Rigby, Idaho, Philo developed a skill in maintaining the family's power generator, and, with encouragement from his father, he found dozens of new uses for electricity. He built motors from spare parts and used them to run his mother's washing machine and some his father's farm machines (Paul Schatzkin, *The Boy Who Invented Television: A Story of Inspiration, Persistence and Quiet Passion* [Silver Spring, Md.: TeamCom Books, 2002], 3). He constructed a telegraph line, connecting his house with the home of a nearby friend. Soon, he was busy wiring homes and barns with electricity. At the request of his bishop, he even wired his church meetinghouse.

Whenever young Philo earned money, he would purchase the latest science magazines and then retreat to his attic to explore the world of science by reading his magazines or any scientific book or journal he could get his hands on. Once while reading, he learned of a national contest to see who could create the best invention to improve the automobile. He rarely rode in the new "horseless carriages," but he came up with an idea to prevent automobiles from being stolen. He invented a special magnetized key that would only start its corresponding car. His invention took top prize!

One of the World's Greatest Thinkers

In 1999, *Time* magazine named Philo Farnsworth one of the one hundred great scientists and thinkers of the twentieth century. During his lifetime he was awarded more than two hundred patents in the field of electronics. Philo's son Kent remembers that his father credited God as the source of his ingenious ideas.

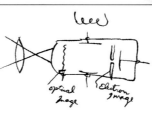

Tolman's Blackboard Sketch

As Philo explained his television system to his high school science teacher, he sketched this diagram of the image dissector—an electronic television camera. His idea consisted of two parts, the image dissector and the cathode-ray tube (television receiver). Inside the image dissector, the picture (image) would be divided up (dissected) into lines and changed into electricity. In the cathode-ray tube, electricity would be changed back into pictures.

Electronic Inspiration

When Philo was young, he dreamed of trapping light in an empty jar and transmitting it one line at a time on a magnetically deflected beam of electrons. This principle still forms the heart of modern television. Though the essence of the idea is extraordinarily simple, it eluded the most prominent scientists of Philo's day.

Although he wanted to pursue his scientific aspirations, Philo assisted his financially struggling family by working on the farm and helping his father plow the fields. One day while chained to a horse-drawn plow and dreaming about television, he halted the horses and looked over the many rows of long, straight furrows of dirt. The field before him appeared as a great picture made of repeated lines. One line did not mean much, but together they created a complete picture. Philo was envisioning a way to transmit vision, line upon line. Each line could be converted into electricity and sent over a distance. At the receiving end, electrical lines could be reassembled into the same pattern and turned again into a complete picture!

Justin Tolman, Philo's science teacher at Rigby High School, was truly amazed at the youngster's grasp of electronics and his ability to solve problems with innovative solutions. One day after school in 1922, Mr. Tolman watched for hours as Philo expertly drew diagrams on the blackboard, illustrating his television theory and explaining how his system would bring pictures of living scenes into the living rooms of America. Philo and Mr. Tolman spent several evenings at the high school blackboard exploring Philo's theory. Mr. Tolman was confident, given the necessary equipment to conduct experiments, that Philo could produce a wonderful invention.

Elma "Pem" Farnsworth

Pem is depicted here on a picture tube in 1931. Her face is tilting away from the camera because of the intense lighting required by the early image dissector. A close examination of the painting shows the raster (scan) lines. Her early appearance on a picture tube may make Elma G. Farnsworth the first television personality. Not long after Philo and Pem met, Philo told her, "Pem, I think we were meant for each other." They were sealed in the Salt Lake Temple on May 27, 1969.

Philo's Love for the Violin

As a young boy, Philo made extra money raising and selling lambs. After patiently saving his money, he was eager to purchase a bicycle from his grandma's Sears catalog. After showing his grandma the bicycle, she suggested that he consider selecting a violin instead. Although a little reluctant at first, Philo purchased a violin with the hopes of someday producing beautiful music. He never regretted his choice, and later he played violin in the school orchestra (McPherson, 12, 13).

It wasn't until several years later, when Philo was married and attending Brigham Young University, that he was able to obtain the financial backing he needed to perfect his television. His initial attempt to broadcast an image resulted in a loud exploding noise and a smoke-filled room. But learning from his trials, he and his lab team finally succeeded in transmitting an image of a line to a four-inch viewing screen. Upon seeing the image, Philo announced excitedly, "That's it folks! We've done it! There you have electronic television!" (Stephanie Sammartino McPherson, *TV's Forgotten Hero* [Minneapolis, Minn.: Carolrhoda Books, 1996], 55).

Later, Philo planned a special demonstration for those who were financially supporting his efforts. One of the backers, eager to make profit from television, often asked when he was going to see some dollar signs from Philo's invention. Philo answered by televising a thick, black dollar sign.

Nearly fifteen years after Philo impressed his science teacher with his television theory, Mr. Tolman recreated Philo's blackboard diagram as part of his testimony in patent litigation between Philo and the giant Radio Corporation of America (RCA). Impressed with Mr. Tolman's clear description of Philo's television, the patent office awarded the patent to the young inventor. Philo eventually won all of his extensive litigation against RCA, becoming the first independent inventor ever awarded a royalty-paying patent license by RCA.

Philo Farnsworth died in 1971 of heart failure following a bout with pneumonia. His scientific theories changed the lives of people around the world. Through his many accomplishments, he proved his favorite saying: "The difficult we do at once; the impossible takes a little longer" (McPherson, 84).

KACEY McCALLISTER

KACEY MCCALLISTER and his family were visiting Roosevelt, Utah, in 1993 to say farewell to an uncle who was leaving on a mission to Dallas, Texas. As the family waited to cross a busy two-lane road, Kacey's older brother and sister crossed the street first. Six-year-old Kacey waited with his parents while two cars passed, then he darted toward his siblings. He never saw the oncoming semi-trailer truck.

Before the ambulance arrived, Kacey lay for twenty minutes on the pavement with two severed femoral arteries—the major arteries in the legs. By the time he was transported to the local hospital, he had no blood pressure. Once he was stabilized, he was flown to Primary Children's Medical Center in Salt Lake City. Kacey spent several months there recovering from his injuries (Laura Dayton, "Kacey McCallister: Unstoppable!" *BFS*, Summer 2002, 55).

"There's no reason he should have lived," said Bernie, Kacey's father. "There is no question that it's a miracle. God just had a greater plan for him and saved him" (Dayton, 55).

Kacey does not recall the accident and never thinks about it unless someone asks. "I can remember the whole day up until then, but I don't remember the impact," he said. "It's just a white flash. I remember

the sound of the helicopter and faces from the hospital. I remember the truck driver coming and giving me a stuffed animal" (Dayton, 55).

Kacey's six-month stay at Primary Children's Medical Center was filled with exercises and rehabilitation to prepare him for his new life without legs. Doctors gave him a wheelchair and fitted him with two artificial legs, which he has never liked because they slow him down. Kacey has described his prostheses as "his prison" because walking with them is slow and difficult (Roy Gault, "Young Athlete Ignores Disability," *Statesman Journal*, 29 March 1998, 6A).

"I don't want to be noted as a kid who's disabled because I'm not," he said. Kacey considers himself to be "a basic, normal American kid" who "can compete as well as anybody, if not better" (Gault, 1A).

Sometimes Kacey has been the target of teasing and cruel jokes at school. But when strangers or kids at school are unkind, he remains polite, said friend Chris Nelson. "When people talk about him or try to put him down, he doesn't mind—doesn't let it get to him," Chris said. "He looks at the bright side of everything. And he treats people the way he wants to be treated" (Gault, 6A).

Kacey always tries to maintain a positive outlook on life because he's decided that it's better to be happy than depressed. Instead of letting the loss of his legs slow him down, he learned how to

Encouraging Others

On many occasions, Kacey has visited elementary schools to talk about his challenges and accomplishments. He teaches students that "disabled" doesn't mean "unable," and he gets satisfaction out of motivating others to raise their levels of accomplishment.

Olympic Moment

"Carrying the Olympic torch was an awesome experience for me," he said of his participation in the Olympic torch relay in early 2002. "For a glorious moment, I was able to be a representative of my church and country. As I look at Olympic photographs from Salt Lake City, I remember the torch that I assisted in bringing there."

use his arms and hands to do everything any other boy can do. While in the sixth grade, he was a two-foot-seven-inch basketball player who could scoot himself quickly across the basketball court.

"He doesn't appear, in his mind, to have any kind of disability," said one coach. "He just goes" (Gault, 1A).

Kacey, who rides a bike, has played organized baseball, snow skied downhill with outriggers, and completed a fifty-mile hike with his Boy Scout troop. As a young man, he would get up at 5:30 every morning to deliver newspapers in his wheelchair.

During the seventh grade, he noticed that his friends enjoyed wrestling. "It seemed like fun: they were doing it, so I joined them" (Dayton, 56). Kacey didn't do well at first, but when he entered high school, he joined the wrestling team and began developing innovative wrestling techniques and strategies.

"Without legs, leverage is a real problem for me," he said. "I have to work around it. I have to get creative."

Although Kacey's style is unorthodox, his upper body strength gives him an advantage in his weight class. Once he gets a good hold on an opponent, the match is all but over. "Kacey is a pit bull," his wrestling coach said. "Once he locks onto you, you are in trouble. He has the upper body of a 171-pounder" (Dan Mooney, "I Can Do Anything . . . ," *The Oregonian*, 29 January 2002, D1). That fact can be daunting for Kacey's opponents because he splits time between the 103- and the 112-pound weight classes.

One of Kacey's wrestling opponents, ranked fifth in the state, said, "Once he gets ahold of you, all you can do is wait for the referee to blow his whistle for a stalemate. He's the strongest guy I've ever wrestled. Kacey McCallister has the biggest heart of any wrestler I've ever seen" (Mooney, D1).

Giving 110 Percent

Kacey's strong spirit and desire to give 110 percent to everything he does is an inspiration to others. One of his coaches said Kacey makes people around him better because when they see him perform, they can't help but think, "Wow, look what this guy's doing with what he has and what I'm doing with what I have" (Gault, 7A). Kacey's principal at McNary High School in Salem, Oregon, said Kacey doesn't ask for anything from anyone. "You see kids complaining about their lot in life, and then there is Kacey," he said (Dayton, 57).

Setting the Pace on and off the Course

Kacey participates in cross-country and track, participating in the 1,500- and 3,000-meter events. Using a special racing chair, he raced to the school's best time in the 3,000. During his high school's state championship football season, he contributed to team spirit by serving as the school's mascot.

Kacey enjoys the same respect from members of his wrestling team, who accept him as just one of the guys. While his teammates run during warm-ups, Kacey keeps up, barreling along on his hands. On the mat during matches, he encourages and roots for his teammates.

Kacey participates in plenty of other activities besides sports. He sings in the school choir, actively participates in Boy Scouts, and enjoys roles in high school drama productions. With a grade-point average above 3.6, Kacey looks forward to attending college after high school. First, however, he plans to serve a mission.

"I believe that every worthy and prepared young man should serve a full-time mission," said Kacey. "I plan on serving when I am nineteen because I know if I didn't, I would be missing out on one of the greatest blessings of my life."

Two of the greatest blessings in Kacey's life have been his faith in the gospel and the strength of his family. "My family has helped me in my adventures by *not* doing everything for me, but they have always been there for me."

A Firm Foundation

"The gospel has assisted me greatly by teaching me how to live my life. I know that I should not swear or take the Lord's name in vain. I want to honor the Word of Wisdom by not drinking alcohol or taking harmful drugs. By living these principles, I have been blessed with both strong body and mind. When a hurdle in life gets shoved in my way, I like to plow over it rather than slow down or take the easy route. When we are faced with stumbling blocks, we should face them with a prayer in our hearts and the scriptures in our hands."

DALE MURPHY

DALE MURPHY wasn't always an all-star. In fact, his athletic career got off to a rocky start. After his parents enrolled him in Little League baseball at age eight, Dale collected a grand total of one hit that first season—not quite what you'd expect from someone who became one the greatest power hitters ever to play baseball. But Dale was determined. He played baseball every summer, demonstrating his early dedication to the sport by drilling holes in bats, filling the holes with lead, and swinging the heavier bats in his basement.

Growing up in Portland, Oregon, Dale enjoyed playing high school football and basketball, but he remained dedicated to baseball. As a high school senior, he was a six-foot-six catcher with a gun for an arm and a .400 batting average. He was the best high school talent in Portland.

The Atlanta Braves drafted Dale in the first round (fifth overall pick) of the June 1974 draft. The adjustment from high school ball to the pros was one of the largest steps Dale ever had to make. All of a sudden everyone was throwing hard and hitting hard.

During spring training in 1975, a few of Dale's teammates frequently discussed religion. He decided that it was time for him to be a better person, to learn more about leading a Christian life, and to become more spiritually centered. But he was not sure where to attend church or how to pray—or even if prayer was important. Some players encouraged him to steer clear of religion because, they said, "It was too strange" (Dale Murphy, *Murph* [Salt Lake City: Bookcraft, 1986], 43).

One evening on the team bus, Dale sat next to a respected teammate, Barry Bonnell, who was reading a book with a blue cover called the Book of Mormon. The men's discussion about The Church of Jesus Christ of Latter-day Saints during the ensuing eight-hour bus ride led to Dale's conversion. Following his baptism, he knew that he wanted to get married in the temple so he could be with his wife and family for eternity.

Dale quickly climbed through the Braves' minor league system, reaching the majors in his third season. Because it's easier for professional athletes to fall in with the wrong crowd than it is to keep high standards, Dale didn't socialize much. After his first major league season, he decided to attend Brigham Young University so he could surround himself with people who shared his values.

Shortly after arriving at BYU, Dale met Nancy Thomas. He soon had a spiritual confirmation that she was the one for him. "I remembered the feeling I had when I prayed about the truthfulness of the Book of Mormon," he said. "It was a very strong feeling, like a burning within me. As I got to know Nancy better, it kept getting stronger and stronger, telling me that she was definitely the right one" (Murphy, 74). Dale and Nancy were married in the Salt Lake Temple a little more than a year after they met.

Dale faced adversity early in his major league career when his throwing arm lost its accuracy. As a catcher, he depended on his throwing arm so he could throw out base runners. Team managers helped him regain his accuracy and find his niche by moving him from catcher to first base, left field, center field, and finally right field, where he remained for the duration of his career. Murphy responded by gunning out numerous runners at the plate and being named a National League all-star.

"I think the greatest honor that can come to a player is to be voted an all-star by baseball fans, and it humbles me when they choose me," Dale said during his career (Murphy, 83).

Serving Others

Before a ball game at Atlanta Fulton County Stadium on June 12, 1983, Dale met a six-year-old girl who had lost both arms and a leg in a power-line accident. The girl's nurse asked Dale if he would hit a home run for her. Dale told the girl, "If I hit one, it will be for you." That night he hit not one but two home runs, driving in all three runs in a 3–2 Braves victory. "One of the most striking memories of my childhood is my mother going to school every day as a volunteer to teach handicapped children," Dale said. "When I asked her why she did it, she replied, 'It's important.' Nothing more needed to be said. She could help someone, so she did. I was always taught that a 'meaningful life' is just that. Society is what we make of it, so we'd better try to make it the best we can" (Peter Gammons, "A Man Who Can't Say No," *Sports Illustrated*, 21 December 1987, 17).

Dale's father used to tell him, "Dare to be good." Dale followed that advice by giving extra effort, taking risks, and daring to be the best ballplayer he could be. His efforts paid off in 1982, when he led the Braves to the play-offs, led the league in runs batted in, won a Gold Glove award, and was named National League Most Valuable Player. Receiving the Gold Glove, given in recognition of defensive excellence, surprised Dale and taught him a lesson: "If you work hard enough you can succeed, even if you end up doing something totally different from what you originally planned. It's a lesson that's helped me in many areas of my life" (Murphy, 118).

Dale won another MVP in 1983, and he eventually became the fifth-highest-paid baseball player ever. He apologetically noted, "Salaries . . . are kind of crazy. I mean, it's not like we are firemen or doctors, people who really do important things."

With the accolades came many autograph seekers. Despite all the praise, Dale believed that he was no different from the individuals seeking his autograph. Witnessing how people look up to ballplayers, he thought it was unfortunate that children don't consider doctors and schoolteachers as heroic as athletes.

During the height of his career, Dale received many requests to make public-service announcements, do fundraising, and make telephone calls to hospitalized children. He enjoyed the chance to help, and he met every request that time allowed. "What's a three-minute call if for three minutes you can make a sick kid forget where he is?" asked Dale (Gammons, 17).

Missionary Service

From 1997–2000, following Dale's retirement, he and his wife, Nancy, presided over the Boston Massachusetts Mission. Dale believes that the best decision a young man can make is to serve a full-time mission—regardless of educational plans or professional oppportunities.

Although Dale was committed to his baseball team, baseball fans, and community service, he recognized that he had eternal responsibilities to his family. "I find when I go to my Heavenly Father for guidance, he helps me make the right decisions to keep my life in balance" (Murphy, 149). Dale said that by concentrating on the most important things in life, he has been able to stay on top of his game—on the field as well as in his faith.

Being a famous member of the Church always placed Dale in the spotlight. But without worrying about the approval of others or his public image, he has lived his life as honorably as he could. "If you live what you believe, you will always have the respect of others," he said (Gammons, 16). Dale's ability to live by his principles while consistently performing with the best players in baseball during his career, from 1974 to 1993, made him an intriguing personality who realized that his talents *are* a gift.

Thoughts for Today's Youth

"If there was one thing I could say, it would be to stay close to your family and to the Church. These may not be the popular teachings of this day, but someday you'll understand. Don't be fooled by those who would knowingly or unknowingly want to change your priorities. Some of those people may even be your friends. Some are definitely not your friends, though, and they'll try to teach you that the gospel is not the best way of life for you. Hang in there! If you aren't sure about it now, I can promise you that someday you will be sure. Kneel and ask your Father in Heaven for help, and he'll give you the strength to overcome your temptations. He'll also guide you toward such important steps as serving a mission and getting married in the temple. I assure you that you won't ever regret doing the right thing" (Murphy, 151).

7

DON LIND

DON LIND was born during the Great Depression to parents who instilled within Don and his siblings the belief that they could do anything they set their minds to do. Although his father was busy providing for his family, he took time to teach Don about the world around him. Before he entered first grade, Don could perform long division, and he had learned about the principles of physics, including the phases of the moon, levers and wedges, and inclined planes.

While he was a sophomore at the University of Utah, Don received a call to serve a mission in New England. He had planned and saved for a mission his entire life, but when the time came to serve, dissenting voices tried to persuade him not to go. He and his debate partner were nationally ranked and had a good chance of winning a national championship. If Don served a mission, his partner would graduate during his absence, and he would lose his chance to compete for a national title.

"In the end, there was really no decision to make, however," Don said. "The decision had been made many years before. . . . I never regretted my choice. In the eternal scheme of things, the mission was where I needed to be right then" (Kathleen Maughan Lind, Don Lind, Mormon Astronaut [Salt Lake City: Deseret Book, 1985], 28).

In 1953, following his mission, Don graduated with high honors in physics from the University of Utah and then signed up for Officers Candidate School in preparation for becoming a navy combat pilot. Following four years in the navy, he returned to school. Soon after he received his doctorate in high-energy nuclear physics in 1964 from the University of California at Berkeley, the Kennedy administration announced the creation of a manned space program. Enthusiastically, Don filled out his astronaut application, only to be turned down because he did not have the required flying hours. He was more hopeful when he turned in his second application because by then he had logged the additional required flying hours as a Naval Reserve pilot. He met all the requirements except one: he was seventy-six days too old. His application was again rejected.

Without giving up, Don prepared for another application and kept himself physically fit by maintaining a strict exercise program. He met all the requirements on his third application, which had no age stipulation. His application was pooled with 3,200 others, including some of the best pilots in the world. But Don's superior physical rating and high qualifications helped him make it to the final selection group of nineteen. His determination not to give up was rewarded in April 1966, when he was accepted as an astronaut in the National Aeronautics and Space Administration program.

As Don was being considered for the astronaut program, he had to be cleared for top-secret work. The FBI thoroughly checked out his background, learning of his character by talking to many people who knew him: friends, neighbors, teachers, and employers.

While reflecting on this investigation, Don commented, "Suppose I had not always been quite honest. Then at some stage of the screening, if a neighbor had said, 'Yes, I remember that Lind boy, he used to steal hubcaps,' that would have been the end. And it would have been no use my protesting that I had done it only for fun. . . . Everything we do in this life counts, because each action adds up to or subtracts from the total person and his strength" (Lind, 14).

The Space Shuttle

Space shuttles are the first vehicles capable, on a routine basis, of being launched into space and returning to earth. Shuttles are used as orbiting laboratories in which scientists and mission specialists conduct a wide variety of scientific experiments. They leave earth and its atmosphere under rocket power and, after their missions, streak back through the atmosphere without flying power and land like a glider.

Don, who flew on the space shuttle *Challenger* just nine months before it exploded after liftoff in January 1986, was saddened when the shuttle *Columbia* broke up on reentry on February 1, 2003. "Astronauts realize there's a risk in flying," he said, but astronauts are willing to take that risk for the benefit of humanity (Elyse Hayes, "Taking a Chance on Every Flight, Utahn Says," *Deseret News*, 2 February 2003, A2).

Blastoff!

"Once we were all settled, it was quiet in the cockpit," Don said of the final moments before liftoff. "Each man's thoughts were his own. As the launch sequence progressed inexorably toward the moment when the engines would be ignited, I was surprised how relaxed I was. When our onboard computer picked up the count at Launch minus thirty-one seconds, I allowed myself a modest measure of emotion. And as the rumble of the main engines began at Launch minus eight seconds, I felt a much larger dose of adrenaline. But when the solid rockets ignited and we surged upward, my emotions gave way to unrestrained elation. We were on our way!" (Lind, cover jacket). Don later added, "It was like going to the circus and getting my Ph.D. and celebrating our oldest child's first birthday and going on my first date all rolled into one."

Don's extensive astronaut education included paramedic training, navy frogman underwater training, desert survival techniques, and jungle survival school. He prepared to fly a lunar landing module by flying helicopters, and he prepared to study the moon's surface by becoming an expert in astrogeology.

After receiving his basic training, Don began working with the Apollo program, which planned to put a man on the moon. He supervised the development of equipment and procedures that crews would use on the moon, and he spent many hours in a pressurized space suit to determine what experiments could be done in the suit.

"I think I probably know more about what Neil Armstrong and Buzz Aldrin were to do on the lunar surface than they did," Don said regarding mankind's historic first visit to the moon, "because I had spent about two and a half years developing all those procedures and working out the tests on the hardware they were to use" (Lind, 114–15).

Don was in the NASA control room during the first moon landing and saw firsthand one of the greatest days in all human history. Reaching the moon was an extremely difficult technological challenge with many setbacks. Commenting on the effort involved, Don said, "If we choose our goals and work toward them earnestly, we can accomplish unbelievable things. But without specific goals, we can spend much energy spinning our wheels and getting nowhere. We might have our own 'fire' of adversity along the way, but if we don't give up, we will achieve the end we are seeking" (Lind, 122).

Don trained for two space missions and was expected to be the sixteenth man to walk on the moon, but his mission was canceled due to budgetary cuts. His hard work

Becoming an Astronaut

As a young boy, Don did not dream of becoming an astronaut because back then there were no astronauts. When young people ask him today how they can begin an astronaut career, there is little he can tell them. That's because the requirements of becoming an astronaut are always changing. Thus, the most important advice Don gives to anyone with a goal is, "Always do your very best. . . . Doing or not doing your best has underlying effects that can make or break the attainment of your goal" (Lind, 13).

eventually paid off, however, when the crew for the Spacelab 3 science mission was announced in February 1982. After nineteen years as an astronaut, Don was finally going into space!

Three years later, on April 29 1985, Don flew to space aboard the space shuttle *Challenger*. As the payload commander, he made the most of every available minute in space by supervising fifteen experiments on board. Because his flight lasted a full week, completing 110 orbits of the earth, he was in orbit on the Sabbath. His bishop gave him permission to observe the Sabbath by having a private sacrament meeting.

One highlight of his trip was gazing upon the earth, alone, from the flight deck. Of that moment, he said, "Throughout my life I have been repeatedly impressed with the grandeur of the Lord's earth, but never as intensely as at that moment. I was glad to be alone. Because of the sheer beauty spread below me, tears came to my eyes" (Lind, 165–66).

Reflecting on his career, Don recognizes that the Lord guided his steps throughout his life. "When I was young, there was no such thing as a space program," he said. "I really didn't know I was preparing for this, but I tried to do my best at whatever I did; then I let the Lord take the lead, to guide me to where I am" (Lind, 35).

The Space Suit

Think about how you suit up when you go outside on a cold winter's day. You put on your long underwear, shirt, pants, sweater, jacket, gloves, hat or hood, scarf, and boots. Now, imagine what you would have to wear to protect yourself from radiation and lack of atmosphere! Outer space is an extremely hostile place. If you were to step outside a spacecraft into space or onto a world with little or no atmosphere, such as the moon or Mars, and you were not wearing a space suit, the following things would happen:

- You would become unconscious within fifteen seconds because of a lack of oxygen.
- Your blood and body fluids would "boil" and then freeze because there is little or no air pressure.
- Your skin and internal organs would expand because of the boiling fluids.
- You would face extreme temperatures. In sunlight the temperature is 248 degrees Fahrenheit; in the shade, it's 148 degrees.
- You would be exposed to various types of radiation, such as cosmic rays and charged particles emitted from the sun (solar wind).
- You could be hit by small particles of dust or rock that move at high speeds (micrometeoroids) or orbiting debris from satellites or spacecraft.

9

LIRIEL DOMICIANO

LIRIEL DOMICIANO and her three sisters were reared by loving parents in a poor suburb in Sao Paulo, Brazil. The four girls and their parents built their small red-block home with their own hands, mixing the concrete and placing blocks one on top of another to form walls. Money was so scarce that it took months to complete a single wall.

Growing up, the four sisters were best friends. When Liriel was three, she and her sisters enjoyed singing along with recordings of classical music. Day after day they would sing and pretend to be famous actresses and singers. By the time she was five, Liriel's ability to sing began to attract attention, especially when she sang—with ease—arias by composers such as Beethoven and Chopin.

"When I was young, my dream was to become a singer, a complete artist," Liriel said. "I sang because I loved to sing."

Always wanting to perfect her talent, she attended singing classes whenever possible. The classes were difficult, but she persisted and always passed them.

When Liriel was thirteen, several of her Catholic girlfriends decided to become nuns. For a while, she thought she might join them. After all, she had grown up in a Christian home and had accepted her parents' moral and spiritual teachings. But when she and her family heard the restored gospel of Jesus Christ, the girls and their mother readily embraced it.

"I wanted a life protected from drinking, smoking, and immorality, and I thought that becoming a nun would be the protection I would need," said Liriel. "When I was baptized, the Holy Ghost, the standards of the Church, and my priesthood leaders became my protection."

Upon her conversion to the Church, Liriel said she experienced much joy.

"I was able to feel the power of the Holy Ghost working with my heart," she said. "I had constant desires to find more truth and to do the right thing, to follow the Spirit. I had a great desire to read the scriptures so I could learn more of the truth. I was hungry for the gospel of Jesus Christ."

Liriel's testimony was her strength as a young woman. She completed four years of seminary and made the commitment to earn her Young Woman medallion. Earning the medallion was one of her highest priorities.

"I earned every award from Beehive to Laurel," she recalled. "This means to me that I am better prepared for temple marriage, for married life, and for a family. I am prepared spiritually. Regardless of your age, when you look at the medallion you have earned, you will reflect on how it has blessed your life."

In June 2001, at age nineteen, Liriel tried out for Sao Paulo's largest televised talent show—a nationally syndicated talent-discovery program. Because her family could not afford to buy her new clothes for her audition, Liriel and her mother made her dresses.

The show's producers had told Liriel not to mention religion as part of her performance, but she wanted everyone to know she was a Latter-day Saint. She was a convert of just three years and was proud to be a member of the Church. Liriel decided to pray about it before her first performance, and as she finished her prayer, she said God led her eyes to her Young Women medallion. The medallion was her answer!

Liriel put the medallion around her neck and wore it to every performance until the end of the competition. With her prayer answered and her medallion on display, Liriel and her tenor singing partner wowed audiences and swayed judges with their stirring duets of romantic classical songs. In the end, they were declared the winners!

Because the show was as widely watched in Brazil as World Cup soccer, Liriel was an instant success, and soon she and her singing partner, Rinaldo Viana, had a recording contract. Their first CD sold one million copies—the sixth highest-selling CD in Brazil's history. Their follow-up CD a year later has also enjoyed phenomenal success, selling nearly 400,000 copies in one month.

Despite her success, Liriel stays close to the Church and encourages others to do the same. She treasures the moments she has to share her testimony in word and song, and she arranges her busy schedule so that she can speak at as many youth firesides as possible.

"I sing to them, and I bear my testimony," Liriel said. "Because there are difficulties everywhere, all around us, I encourage them to continue to believe and to never fall away. Even in the Church there are difficulties, and I always tell them never to forget that God sent us here to be tested. Our trials are for our growth, and we should not become disillusioned."

Wearing Modest Fashions
Television producers have often encouraged Liriel to "wear clothes that were in style but were not modest," she explained. "I have never fallen off the line regarding my standards. I've always said that my style of dresses is a classic style, and I am not going to change. I am not going to compromise my standards. Even though there is a lot of resistance, even though the people involved in the show frequently criticize me, I have never stepped down from my high standards. I've always persisted and the Lord has opened up the doors. The major part of the people who see me on television praise me a lot, not only for the way I sing but also for the way I look. They say I transmit peace to them, and this helps them to have more hope in life." At the end of 2002, the Brazilian national list of "The Best" listed Liriel as one of the ten best-dressed people in the nation. She was excited to be on this list because she has always made it a point to dress according to Church standards.

While Liriel continues to perform to adoring fans in Brazil, her popularity is spreading throughout the world, including Europe, where she has also performed. Brazilian music executives recognize that she has the potential of becoming one of Brazil's finest lyrical sopranos of all time. A specialist in lyrical music who evaluated Liriel's voice said, "Liriel is extremely talented and is being polished like a fine diamond."

Liriel enjoys the attention, but her long-term goals remain solidly founded in gospel principles. "Five years from now I would like to be married," she said. "I'd like to start a family when I am twenty-five. In ten years, I want to be a complete professional lyrical soprano. To accomplish this, I will practice even more. After I complete all of those things, I want to work full time for the Lord and prepare for his Second Coming. He is calling me. He needs my help in bringing his children to him. I know I am going to have the opportunity to be with my family forever. I am going to participate in the good things in life. Things in life actually are very simple, and it's only necessary for us to learn how to execute our work, and the Lord will make up the differences."

The Importance of Scripture Study
"My family always helps me to have vision. Even when I was very small, I always read the scriptures. I wasn't a member of the Church, but I always wanted to know about God, be near and feel close to him."

Singing with Purpose
"I sing for the Lord, not for money. He gave me my voice, and I will use it to glorify him."

CODY HANCOCK

CODY HANCOCK was crowned world bull-riding champion by the Professional Rodeo Cowboys Association in late 2000. He had entered the National Finals Rodeo in the fifteenth and final qualifying slot. Rising from fifteenth to champion had never been accomplished in bull riding before. Cody's lifelong dream had been fulfilled.

Born in Taylor, Arizona, Cody comes from a long family chain of cowboys. His great-grandfather started the first rodeo in his home-town, and his father is a professional bull rider. When Cody was thirteen, he gave his father a unique Father's Day gift—he paid the entry fee for his dad to compete in a bull-riding contest, which he won.

Through the years, Cody and his father found ways to live gospel standards amid the traditionally rowdy rodeo crowd. As they would travel long distances to participate in rodeos, they often talked about the devastating effects of drinking, smoking, and using drugs. They each had friends whose lives had been destroyed by bad choices. Cody chose to follow in his dad's footsteps, both in riding bulls and in living gospel standards (Sarah Jane Weaver, "Bull Riding Champ Achieves 'Impossible' as Final's Underdog," *Church News*, 17 February 2001, 11).

Cody developed his masterful bull-riding skills through his lifelong pursuit of becoming a bull rider. "Since I was three, all I have ever wanted to be was a bull rider," he said. "My dad rode bulls, and I thought about it all the time. That is one of the reasons I have accomplished what I have."

From age ten to fourteen, Cody often trained for bull riding by looking in the mirror. As he looked at his reflection, he would pretend he was riding a bull and imagine how he would move if the bull twisted to the right or left, or if it jumped or reversed direction. For hours Cody practiced and studied his form and balance. "Now when the bull moves," he said, "my body moves instinctively because I have trained it to do so."

As a teenager, Cody wrote many of his goals in his copy of the Book of Mormon, including becoming a professional bull rider *and* a full-time missionary for the Church (Weaver, 11). In 1994, in order to prepare to achieve his missionary goal, Cody turned down an opportunity to travel the professional rodeo circuit with the then-current world champion. A short time later, he found himself in the Pennsylvania Philadelphia Mission, where he served honorably for two years. After his mission, he needed a year to regain the top physical condition required of champion bull riders. Cody credits the discipline he learned as a missionary for providing him with the necessary strength and focus to excel in his sport.

"After my mission, I was so much more mentally prepared for the travel, being away from my family, the business side of the sport, and everything else that goes with riding bulls," he recalls. "Honoring Church standards has made me a better bull rider because when I am on the road I stay focused on riding bulls and do not get sidetracked with things I shouldn't."

Following his mission, Cody had difficulty paying travel and entry fees on the professional circuit. At times he worried that he might have to give up full-time rodeo. But he stayed focused on his dream and endured the physical and mental challenges of riding at least 125 bulls a year. As a result, his bull-riding marks steadily improved until, during 1999, he was ranked either first or second in the world.

That same year, his dominating rodeo season came to quick halt when a

Mental Toughness

"So much of bull riding is mental. You do not have time to think when that bull jumps out of the gate and is twisting under you to the right or left. If you have time to think, you are already bucked off. Something must already be programmed in your mind. I think that is what has helped me because that is what I have thought about and lived everyday of my life. When the bull spins right, my mind automatically tells my body to move in the same direction. Sometimes I fall off the slower, easier bulls because their slower movements give me time to think. And when I think, I get bucked off. I ride the more difficult bulls the best."

Boyhood Dreams

Although he realized early on that "all I ever wanted to be was a world champion bull rider," Cody earned Eagle Scout, loved baseball, played football, and wrestled at Snowflake High School in Snowflake, Arizona (Jeff Metcalfe, "The Ride of His Life," *Arizona Republic*, 2 December 2001, S2).

bull stepped on and broke his ankle. Five weeks later, Cody was back on the rodeo circuit, but because of the unfortunate accident, he just barely missed qualifying for the National Finals Rodeo. Fifteen riders qualified; Cody placed sixteenth.

"That was the hardest thing in my world at the time—to miss my dream by such a small margin," he said. "But it actually helped me out a lot by putting a fire in me the next year."

Cody returned to bull riding in 2000 more determined than ever. This time, his hard work and perseverance brought him a world championship. In his acceptance speech after winning the title, he thanked his father for teaching him what kind of man to be.

"My dad promised me that if I would go on a mission, rodeo would come a lot easier when I got home. I never really comprehended that until December 2000. Winning a world title was a direct blessing for doing what I am supposed to do," he told the *Church News,* adding that the Church has helped him to stay spiritually focused (Weaver, 11).

During the 2001 season, Cody broke a bull-riding scoring record that had stood for twenty-four years. In the tenth round of the

National Finals Rodeo, he rode a bull named "Mr. USA" nearly to perfection, tallying a score of ninety-six and besting the 1976 NFR record by one point.

Today, in addition to his busy rodeo schedule, Cody makes time to serve in Church callings and is a member of the advisory committee for the Cowboys Against Tobacco. Rather than attend most post-rodeo events, he spends his spare time with his wife, Rinda—whom he married in the Mesa Arizona Temple—and his daughter, Tyree.

Cody credits his wife and family for his success. "My wife deserves the world championship as much or more than I do," he said. "She helps me when I am home and supports me when I am gone, and my mom and dad have sacrificed for me ever since I was little. My whole family has done a lot for my career."

Bull-Riding Rules

A bull rider is not required to spur the bull, but spurring adds points to a rider's score. Upper body control and strong legs are essential to riding bulls. The rider tries to remain forward, or "over his hand," at all times. Leaning back could cause him to be whipped forward when the bull bucks. Judges watch for good body position, use of the free arm, and spurring action. As with all riding events, half of the score in bull riding is determined by the contestant's performance while the other half is based on the animal's efforts. Bull riders are disqualified if they touch the bull, themselves, or the rope with their free hand.

Cody's Tips on Bull Riding

- Try your hardest.
- Have a game plan and be prepared when you sit on a bull.
- Have an instinctive countermove for every move a bull makes.
- Keep moving, stay loose, and be ready for anything.
- Stay focused.

When Cody rides a bull, he is so focused that he seldom hears the cheering crowd. "Sometimes if I have a really great ride, I can begin to hear the crowd toward the end of the ride," he said. "It is unbelievable how long eight seconds last when you're riding a bull. Sometimes it seems like forever, but when you get bucked off you find out that you were still two seconds from getting a whistle."

GAIL S. HALVORSEN

GAIL S. HALVORSEN grew up during the Great Depression on small farms in Utah and Idaho. During the spring, he would labor ten hours a day, six days a week, thinning sugar beets. The monotony of thinning the seemingly endless rows of beets day after day was occasionally broken by the sound of aircraft.

"The sight of a silver shaft against that beautiful blue western sky and the sound that kept it there sent a shiver down my spine each time the event was repeated," Gail explained. Although his hands were hard at work thinning beets, his mind was "free, flying through the blue of the sky and around the white, puffy clouds, stopping in faraway places with strange-sounding names."

Gail's opportunity to become a pilot came in 1940, when the United States increased pilot-training programs in preparation for its inevitable involvement in World War II. Of 120 applicants in Utah, Gail was one of ten accepted into the flight-training program. Until the conclusion of the war, he was assigned to fly foreign transport missions in the South Atlantic Theater.

Following the war, defeated Germany and its capital, Berlin, were carved into four pieces by the conquering allied countries. The Soviet Union controlled the eastern sector of Berlin as well as East Germany. Great Britain, the United States, and France controlled the three western sectors of Berlin as well as West Germany. The four allies ruled in peace until June 24, 1948, when the Soviet Union tried to drive the western allies out of West Berlin by blockading the city. Because Berlin was 110 miles within Russia's controlled territory, Soviet leader Joseph Stalin simply had to blockade the one road, railroad, and canal routes to and from the city in order to cut off food, coal, and other supplies from reaching West Berliners. Rather than free the citizens of West Berlin with guns and tanks, British and American forces began the Berlin airlift—one of the greatest humanitarian missions in the world's history.

To keep more than two million West Berliners alive, 4,500 tons of food, coal, and other essential supplies had to arrive by plane daily! The mission's challenges included terrible weather, short runways, tired pilots, flights over hostile territory, harassment by Russian planes, and mechanical problems. Although he longed to return home after the war, Lt. Gail Halvorsen agreed to serve in this effort, which the Americans called "Operation Vittles." Now, rather than fighting against the Germans, the Americans were dedicating their all to save the Berliners!

One day while in West Berlin, Gail noticed a group of about thirty children gathered to watch the cargo planes swoop out of the sky to land. As he approached the barbed wire fence that separated the curious children from the military base, the young Berliners, in their school-taught English, asked questions about the planes and their lifesaving cargo.

"I received a lesson about priorities," said Gail. "I was astonished with the maturity and clarity that they exhibited in advising me of what their values were and what was of greatest importance to them in these circumstances. The children said, 'During the winter, when the weather is too bad for you to bring enough food into this city, don't worry about us. We can live on very little.' Those who had parents or a single parent or only brothers or sisters all believed that someday there would be enough to eat, but if they lost their freedom they feared they would never get it back. Being more concerned about freedom than flour taught me to be more grateful for whatever I have, especially freedom."

Needing to return to his duties, Gail bade them farewell and walked away, pondering the lessons learned from his new friends. Longing to provide the children with some kind of gift, he instinctively reached into his pocket and found two sticks of gum. He glanced over his shoulder to see the children pressed against the fence, waving good-bye. He then returned, regretting that he could only provide a small offering. He broke the two sticks in half and handed them to a lucky few.

Anxious Anticipation

In 1998, at an air show in Berlin, an emotional sixty-year-old man approached Gail and said, "Fifty years ago I was a boy of ten on my way to school. The clouds were very low with a light rain. Suddenly, out of the mist, came a parachute with a fresh Hershey chocolate bar from America. It landed right at my feet. I knew it was happening but could not believe it was for me. It took me a week to eat that candy bar. The chocolate was wonderful, but it wasn't the chocolate that was important. What it meant was that someone in America knew I was here, in trouble, and needed help. That parachute was something more important than candy; it represented hope—hope that someday we would be free."

Comforting Those in Need of Comfort

During the Berlin airlift, a polio hospital in West Berlin was full of children suffering from severe limited mobility. They wrote letters to Gail, telling him that they had been unable to run or walk after the parachutes and asking him for a favor. "The main point they all wanted to make was for me to disregard the 'quiet' sign on the streets outside the hospital. The doctors had promised it would be okay to fly low over the hospital and drop the goodies in the yard." Soon thereafter, Gail made the requested deliveries in person. "If my heart had been full before, it was now overflowing with the reaction and spirit of these marvelous young people who 'couldn't chase a parachute.'"

Serving and Bringing Joy to Others

"A principle that is essential to my happiness in life is service before self," Gail said. "My father taught me that good things would happen if you did something for someone without expecting anything in return. How is it that the little things in life can provide the most joy and the greatest blessings? Service to others, as the Savior taught, provides those magical moments. The exhortation to serve and to love is so simple, but its blessing is so complex."

"I had never witnessed such an expression of surprise, joy, and sheer pleasure that I beheld in the eyes and faces of those four young people," Gail said. "Nor do I remember seeing such disappointment as was evident in the eyes of those who came so close" to receiving gum.

The gum's foil and wrapper were carefully passed around, and the eyes of the recipients grew large as they smelled the scent of the precious wrapper. "My eyes were sending me a message that my brain couldn't understand," said Gail. "What an impact from just a tiny piece of wrapper. What I could do with thirty full sticks of gum!"

Gail then received a flash of inspiration. He promised the children that on his next day's mission, he would drop gum and chocolate to them from his plane. The children would be able to distinguish his plane from the others because he would wiggle the plane's wings back and forth several times as he approached. Gail kept his promise and began what was to be known as "Operation Little Vittles."

Lieutenant Halvorsen soon became better known as "Uncle Wiggly Wings," the "Chocolate Flyer," and the "Berlin Candy Bomber." His efforts developed into a worldwide mission of love. Businesses, communities, and individuals from around the globe contributed to the worthy effort. At the operation's peak, 850 pounds of small, candy-tied parachutes were shipped to Germany every other day! When Lieutenant Halvorsen left Berlin, he'd flown 126 airlift missions, and his squadron had dropped more than 250,000 parachutes loaded with more than twenty tons of chocolate and gum to Berlin's one hundred thousand children.

"This is an example of little things making a difference in lives," said Gail. "In my case, sharing two sticks of gum changed my life and had an impact on the lives of many in Berlin. This is an example of what my parents taught me in my youth—'by small and simple things are great things brought to pass'" (Alma 37:6).

After his retirement, Gail continued to give others hope through service. He has flown candy to refugee camps in Bosnia, Albanians fleeing from Kosovo, and many children's hospitals. And he has served Church missions in London, England, and St. Petersburg, Russia.

The Priceless Blessing of Freedom
"American youth need to understand how precious and unique our freedoms are. The right to choose for one's self is inherent in every individual regardless of nationality. When that right is taken away, you then realize how precious it is," Gail said. "Likewise, we lose our personal freedom by trying addictive substances like smoking or harmful drugs. By trying these substances just once, we may lose the ability to direct our life. The little decisions in life determine where we will end up. Today, the lure of harmful drugs leads many to miss both their present and long-term goals and even steals their ability to retain their freedom, their moral agency."

LIZ SHROPSHIRE

LIZ SHROPSHIRE was en route to the home of one of her piano students in 1999 when she heard a radio report about Kosovo refugees suffering in the aftermath of ethnic cleansing by Serbian forces. The Serbs had annihilated villages and committed horrific atrocities against unarmed civilians, including children.

The disturbing news report moved Liz to action. She cancelled a vacation to Austria, put her teaching career in Los Angeles on hold, and began a campaign to aid the children of Kosovo.

"I thought, instead of going on vacation for me, I could go help instead," she explained. After consulting with a friend, Liz decided to go to the distraught region and do what she does best: teach music. Within a year, she founded The Shropshire Music Foundation in Gjakova, Kosovo.

Music has been an intricate part of Liz's life since early childhood. While in the fourth grade, the world of music seemed to open for her when she began playing the flute in her school's band program. In addition to studying flute, she began playing the piano, drums, and guitar. Before graduating from high school, she had added the oboe and several percussion instruments to her repertoire.

Liz furthered her music education at Brigham Young University, receiving a bachelor's degree in music composition and theory, and at the University of Southern California, receiving a graduate degree in composition for the music industry. Her experience as an educator includes teaching emotionally disturbed school students in Los Angeles, offering private musical instruction, and serving as the educational director for the Long Beach Symphony.

In preparation for serving the children of Kosovo, Liz gathered more than five thousand dollars worth of donated instruments and music. Upon arriving in Kosovo, she immediately met with children who suffered nightmares from their ordeal. Many children acted aggressively and were unable to concentrate in school. Others were homeless, living in makeshift shelter camps or tents behind their destroyed homes.

Liz went to work organizing her curriculum, which included training local youth volunteers and schoolteachers. She feels that every aspect of the program was inspired by her Heavenly Father.

"There have been so many times I would work out how to teach something or develop a new program," she said. "Then I would pray about my idea, and before I would get off my knees I would have a completely different way to accomplish my objective. The new way would be much more effective and reach many more kids." The result was the creation of the Kosovo Children's Music Initiative, which uses music to help children heal from their war experiences.

"The need for these children to choose peace with their lives rather than hatred is very real," Liz said. "We are helping these children to realize that there is hope, that there is a future, that although they can't control many things in their world, they can control themselves. As children learn to play music, they learn the values of discipline, self-worth, and accomplishment while having fun."

She said her goal is for the children to know that they always have the power to make their own choices, that the path of peace leads to happiness and security, that weapons do not equal power and safety, and that violence is not the answer to their problems.

"Sometimes a song can give us the strength to turn away from that which is wrong," Liz said. "Our goal is for these children to become instruments of peace."

The Importance of Selecting Good Music

Liz enjoys listening to popular music, but she recognizes that careful discretion should be used when selecting music. "The Spirit and common sense can tell you immediately if you should not be listening to a song," she said. "You do not need to listen to the whole song to know that it is not good. Just turn it off! In addition to Church-related music, I really believe that there is enough wonderful music in the world that you do not need to resort to the bad stuff."

The response from the children has been overwhelming. Liz and her staff have taught more than five thousand eager children in classrooms that are often overflowing.

Teachers have noticed that the children who attend Liz's music program perform better in all other classes. One of the many lives she has reached and blessed is a Kosovar boy named Lum.

"His father's dead," Liz said. "He's still living in a shelter camp for people who lost their homes during the war. He has a mother—a good mother—but she hasn't had a home for a really long time."

Lum's mother and teachers could do little to keep him calm and under control. "I couldn't even teach a class without him being extremely disruptive," Liz recalled. She worked constantly with him in her singing and harmonica classes, giving him responsibilities and positive feedback to build his self-worth and make him feel in control of something.

"Now he is one of my best students, and I would trust him with anything," Liz said. "One of his schoolteachers told his mother that Lum used to be her biggest problem, but now he keeps all the other kids quiet. He was even voted class president last year."

The Kosovo Children's Music Initiative has grown more than Liz ever dreamed. "We are running many programs for children. Our youth volunteer program, in which the youth teach and take complete responsibility for music classes, has opened a new level of influence in the community and in the lives of young people that is miraculous. Truly, this program is a miracle and a gift from Heavenly Father, and I am so grateful that he has allowed me the opportunity to be a part of it."

In addition to sharing the gift of music, Liz has found many opportunities to introduce hope through the gospel of Jesus Christ. As one of the only Latter-day Saint voices in Kosovo, Liz frequently utilizes

The Value of Playing an Instrument

"Children should learn how to play an instrument because it opens up the mind in a way that nothing else can," Liz said. "It turns on a part of the soul, a part that would otherwise not be turned on at all. When children start to play music, they open up a part of themselves that will remain open and enrich them for the rest of their lives."

missionary skills learned while she served a full-time mission in Halifax, Nova Scotia.

Her efforts to build the Church have not stopped at giving away copies of the Book of Mormon and teaching missionary discussions. Working under the guidance of the Albanian and Slovenian mission presidents, she has taught new-member discussions and basic gospel classes, and she has helped organize Sunday meetings. She even e-mails reports to the mission presidents on progress and developments.

With faithful optimism, Liz said, "Almost everyone I have spoken to about the Book of Mormon and the tenets of the Church has been receptive. They appear to me to be ready for the gospel, and I believe that many would embrace it if given the opportunity. I recently received a copy of a family home evening manual in Albanian, and immediately I received requests for copies of it."

Liz is not sure how long she will continue her work in Kosovo, but for now she teaches classes six days a week and in her spare time visits shelter camps where people still live in terrible conditions. "Sometimes I'll get home at midnight and realize I haven't eaten anything since early that morning," she said. "It's exhausting, but it's great."

Liz hopes to take her program to other countries where children are suffering the consequences of war. But the future, she said, is in the hands of Heavenly Father, who has guided her work from the beginning. "Everything I have done in my life was just preparing me to be able do this work," she said. "I feel so blessed that Heavenly Father lets me do this."

Assisting in a Worthy Cause

Since 1999, the non-profit Kosovo Children's Music Initiative has provided free musical instruments, musical instruction, and performances for more than five thousand children in war-torn Kosovo. KCMI graciously accepts contributions, including new and used band and orchestra instruments, guitars, and accordions that are in good working condition. For more information, or to donate, contact Shropshire Music Foundation at 1123 East Torreon Drive, Litchfield Park, AZ, 85340, or visit www.teachingchildrenpeace.com.

Precious Joy Found in Serving Others

Liz knows firsthand the joy that comes from serving and assisting others. "Service is like eating healthily," she said. "When you are not eating right and you just want to eat junk food, you think you are happy but you don't really feel that good. And then, when you start eating healthy foods you start to feel so much better; you are happier and life is great. Then you ask yourself, 'Why haven't I been eating right all along?' Service is like that. When you finally get around to serving others you realize how wonderful it is, and you wish you had been more active in serving all along."

PETER VIDMAR

PETER VIDMAR, the youngest of six children, grew up in a home in Los Angeles where he was taught the value of hard work. His parents also taught him and his siblings to never give up and to never complain. These core principles have blessed Peter throughout his gymnastics career as well as throughout his life.

Peter began serious gymnastics training before he entered high school, but he led a fairly normal life. He hung out with friends, attended Church youth activities, and spent many mornings surfing at local beaches.

At age eleven, Peter responded to a newspaper ad and began training with Makoto Sakamoto, who would be his coach for twelve years. By the time Peter turned thirteen, his talents looked so promising that his coach asked him to commit to training seven days a week.

"I was in love with gymnastics and dreamed daily of going to the Olympics," Peter said. "But I told him no. For me, Sunday was the Sabbath, and I didn't engage in recreational activities or sports on Sunday. Not being of my faith, he didn't appreciate that I would refuse extra training time."

Thinking that Peter was showing less than 100 percent commitment, his coach asked him to leave. "I was devastated," Peter said, "but I knew I needed to keep this commandment."

A few weeks later, Makoto met with Peter and his parents. Understanding how committed Peter was to the principle of Sabbath observance, the coach allowed Peter to return—with the understanding that he would train so hard Monday through Saturday that he would truly earn his day of rest!

Because gymnastics is not a mainstream sport, Peter learned firsthand that being a gymnast in high school was not cool. Even after he made the U.S. National Team, no one his age attended his meets. He remembers being on the way to the gym when one of his classmates said, "So, are you going to work out in your pajamas again today, Peter?" Despite such remarks, Peter resolved not to get bogged down by what others thought of him.

"We can spend a lot of time in life comparing ourselves with others," he said. "The problem is we're always going to find someone who is better or smarter or taller or nicer looking or who dresses better. Comparing ourselves with others can be dangerous. It sets up conditions ripe for dangerous choices, disappointment, and defeat. It's only when we compare ourselves to our potential that we lay the foundation for contentment and success."

Peter never experimented with drugs or alcohol. As an athlete, he valued his health. Even more important, he was committed to living the Word of Wisdom. In 1981, during a prestigious gymnastics competition in Europe, he won the vault event. Victorious, he took his place on the center podium and received a gold medal, flowers, and gifts.

After the crowd had cheered, Peter was presented with a silver cup full of wine. He candidly explained that he did not drink. "Then just take a sip and hand it to the next person," he was told. Peter responded, "No, it is against my religion, and I can't even take a sip." When the cup was

Blessings of the Gospel

"As a member of the Church, I have been taught from my youth to live a certain way that seems outdated to many people," Peter said. "But I don't feel hemmed in or burdened by rules. I feel free. I made an ironclad commitment to be married in the temple."

Peter and his wife, Donna, were married in the Los Angeles California Temple in July 1983. He said his temple marriage is more precious to him than all the gold in the world. "When I die, the medals will stay here but the relationship with my wife will go on for eternity. As a parent, I enjoy seeing my children grow when they understand a principle that was taught by the Savior and then put it into action. I have a lot to learn and much more to do, but I have found great peace in my life as a member of the Church of Jesus Christ."

again insistently forced toward Peter, he took it, held it high in the air, and, without taking a sip, passed it to the next person amid the laughter of the crowd.

"It was an awkward and embarrassing moment, but it was easy to say no because I had committed myself to avoid alcohol," Peter said. "There is nothing in the scriptures that guarantees that keeping the commandments will be fun or exciting, and that is okay. In a challenging moment you might feel awkward or embarrassed, but for the long time that follows the experience you will feel good because you did what the Lord expected you to do.

"The opposite is also true. If I had taken a sip of wine, for that brief moment it would have appeared that I had solved my problem. I would not have embarrassed myself in front of thousands of people, and no one would have laughed at me. However, for a long time after that I would have carried with me the remorse of knowing I compromised my beliefs."

A defining moment in Peter's gymnastics career came during the world championships in Budapest, Hungary, a few months before the 1984 Summer Olympics in Los Angeles. In second place going into the finals of the high bar, Peter was fine-tuning his Olympic routines. Wanting to win a gold medal, he planned a particularly difficult maneuver. He began his routine, did a half turn, straddled his legs, and performed a back flip. When he came back down to catch the bar, he fell nine feet onto the mat. He remounted and finished his routine.

"Everything is a learning experience," his coach told him. From then on, Peter resolved to work overtime on the high bar. "The next time the heat was on, I did not want to fail," he said. "For the next eight months, there wasn't a workout that didn't include an extra session, or two, working on that maneuver—a double release.

Pommel Horse

Many people consider the pommel horse the most difficult of all men's gymnastics events. Imagine relying on the muscles you use to hoist yourself up on the kitchen counter, and you'll get an idea of why this event is so tough. Gymnasts must perform an "element of value" on both ends of the horse while executing continuous circular movements, interrupted only by required scissor elements. The hands are the only part of the body that should touch the horse, and the entire routine must flow with steady, controlled rhythm. If gymnasts get in trouble on the horse, they must continue moving through the routine while making corrections. The basic skills needed on the pommel horse require twice as long to master as the skills required in other gymnastics events.

Mind Games

While training for the Olympics, Peter and his training partner, Tim Daggett, would play mind games to maintain focus and motivation during seemingly endless routines. "We'd imagine ourselves actually competing in the Olympic Games—not just competing sometime during the meet, but at the conclusion, when all the pressure was on and the outcome was up to us. We'd imagine the ultimate gymnastics scenario and put ourselves smack in the middle of it. The empty training gym became an Olympic arena with thousands in the seats and millions watching on television. My heart would start to pound, I would forget how tired I was, and I would perform my routine. When the day came that I was actually in the Olympic finals, I imagined I was back in the quiet gym."

I never liked doing it because I frequently crashed, but I did it anyway."

By the time the 1984 Olympics arrived, Peter was ready. He successfully completed the difficult high bar maneuver on his way to a perfect routine, scoring a 10! Peter also captained the U.S. Men's Gymnastics Team to its first-ever Olympic gold medal. No one ever expected the U.S. men's team to beat the perennial dictators of the sport—the Chinese and Japanese. So when the team mounted the center podium, the hometown crowd went berserk, roaring and waving American flags! "Imagine a rock concert and the last day of school rolled into one," Peter said of that memorable moment.

Peter credits many people for helping him achieve his Olympic dream, including one person in particular. "I was grateful to my Father in Heaven for blessing me with all that led to that moment on the victory stand," he said.

During those same games, Peter also captured the gold medal in the pommel horse, scoring another perfect 10, and he became the first American to take the silver in the individual all-around men's competition. He missed the gold in the all-around by only twenty-five thousandths of a point, making that competition the closest battle in Olympic history.

With winning performances averaging 9.89, Peter is the highest scoring U.S. male gymnast in Olympic history. In 1998, he was inducted into the International Gymnastics Hall of Fame.

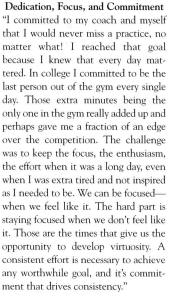

Dedication, Focus, and Commitment

"I committed to my coach and myself that I would never miss a practice, no matter what! I reached that goal because I knew that every day mattered. In college I committed to be the last person out of the gym every single day. Those extra minutes being the only one in the gym really added up and perhaps gave me a fraction of an edge over the competition. The challenge was to keep the focus, the enthusiasm, the effort when it was a long day, even when I was extra tired and not inspired as I needed to be. We can be focused—when we feel like it. The hard part is staying focused when we don't feel like it. Those are the times that give us the opportunity to develop virtuosity. A consistent effort is necessary to achieve any worthwhile goal, and it's commitment that drives consistency."

ARIEL BYBEE

ARIEL BYBEE always wanted to be a singer. As a six-year-old girl, she still remembers her parents taking her into a dark theater during a performance. "I was immediately captivated by every aspect of the environment. I just loved it," she said. "Ever since, I have always been drawn to that kind of a setting."

Ariel was reared in Southern California, the third child in a family of five children. Her mother's singing talents, combined with her father's experience in teaching music, created a natural setting for Ariel's talents to flourish. Throughout her life, she has been drawn to classical music, singing, and theater. Born with extraordinary singing ability, she sought every opportunity to sing and perform on stage.

Achieving good grades was a challenge for Ariel while in elementary school. She was born with an eye condition that hindered her ability to read. Corrective eye surgery in the fifth grade, coupled with additional academic effort, enabled her to improve her grades and reading skills.

While attending Brigham Young University as a freshman in 1960, Ariel auditioned for the opera *Rigoletto*. Though she had never seen an opera previously, she was awarded the principal role of Maddalena, who appears in the fourth and final act. "When people ask me about the first opera I saw, I tell them it was the first three acts of *Rigoletto*," Ariel recalls. "That is how I got the bug. Just one opera and I loved it so much I knew this was where I belonged."

A few years following her college graduation, she performed in the Utah Opera Company's production of *Madame Butterfly*. One day during rehearsals, she and her boyfriend were visiting a park in Provo Canyon when an electrical power line supplied with 7,500 volts of electricity fell on them. They both suffered severe burns, but miraculously neither died. With bandages on her feet and arms, Ariel performed the starring role of Madame Butterfly.

When she was twenty-six, Ariel traveled to New York City to participate in the final round of the Metropolitan Opera Auditions. She was disappointed that she did not win, but the experience taught her a valuable lesson.

"I realized right then that if I wanted to compete with the people who regularly sing at the Met—with the famous opera singers of the world—I needed to go back to the drawing board and work a lot harder."

During the next three years of strenuous practice, singing was not very satisfying for Ariel. Before her experience at the Met, singing had been relatively fun and easy, but Ariel realized that if she wanted to sing among the best in the world, music would have to become work. So she increased her study of music and spent countless lonely hours in practice rooms working on her vocal technique. In addition to perfecting her vocal skills, Ariel worked with coaches on interpretation, style, and language, learning to sing well in English, Italian, French, German, Russian, and even Czechoslovakian.

She left Utah 1968 to perform with the San Francisco Opera Company, and while there she was offered a contract with the Metropolitan Opera in New York. During her eighteen seasons at the Met, Ariel sang in 470 performances,

Appreciating Classical Music

"I suppose I have always appreciated classical music because I grew up with it around me all the time. If you do not have that influence, it's worth the effort to expose yourself to it. Exposure to classical music will trigger emotions within you that will cause you to say, 'Oh my goodness, that is so wonderful and exciting. Why haven't I been drawn to this before?' A young man came up to me recently and said, 'I never thought I liked opera until I attended a concert of operatic arias at your home a few years ago. Now I go regularly with my parents to Chicago to attend the opera.'

"I believe that we are naturally drawn to that which is good, including good classical music. But we need to allow ourselves to be exposed to it and perhaps even to learn about it. If you make the effort and give classical music a chance, it can change your life for the better.

"For a singer, learning to become a great opera singer is something like an athlete preparing for the Olympics. You have to be in constant training. Opera singers are 'vocal athletes.' They have to learn to sing higher, lower, louder, softer, and prettier than anyone else. They have to be able to produce a good-sized voice that is able to carry over a seventy-five-piece orchestra without a microphone."

often covering (understudying) famous singers and singing principal roles such as Hansel in *Hansel and Gretel*.

While in New York, she lived with her husband and daughter across the street from Lincoln Center, where the Met is located, and near the Church's Manhattan chapel. Among other callings in her Manhattan Ward, Ariel served as Relief Society president and Primary president.

"Certainly everyone knew at the Metropolitan Opera that I was a member of the Church, and they respected me for my strong religious convictions," she said. "I was never asked to do anything to compromise my standards. It was a blessing working at the Met because they never rehearsed or had a performance on Sunday. I let people know that my church was right across the street and that it was as important to me as anything I was doing in my life."

The gospel blessed Ariel and her family as she performed throughout the world. Wherever they traveled, the first thing they did upon arrival was locate the nearest chapel.

"We always made a point to visit the local chapels and temples," Ariel said. "Going to church in other countries has always given me an incredible sense of security. No matter where you are in the world, the one constant is the Church. Going to church, partaking of the sacrament, and singing the hymns, regardless of language, always made me feel like I was home."

The highlights of her career center on singing sacred and classical music, which can have a spiritual effect on both singer and listener. Singing such music gives Ariel an opportunity to bear her testimony. One of her many memorable experiences occurred during the premier of the Mozart opera *La Clemenza di Tito*.

"Mozart's music is as spiritual as any music I have ever sung," she said. "I remember singing in an opening-night performance that transported me. The evening was over, and I didn't even remember it."

Other spiritual highlights of Ariel's career include singing for President Gordon B. Hinckley on numerous occasions, including his ninetieth birthday celebration. She said she will always remember singing "Faith in Every Footstep" at President Hinckley's request during the dedication of the Winter Quarters Nebraska Temple in April 2001.

"Singing a solo in the celestial room prior to President Hinckley's dedication of the temple was one of the most powerful moments of my life," she said. "The opportunity to sing in the temple brought together all of the most important aspects of who I am into one moment."

Following her retirement from the Met, Ariel became an artist-in-residence at the University of Nebraska–Lincoln School of Music. She directs opera, teaches master classes and voice lessons, and participates in outreach and recruiting activities.

Ariel's Testimony

"I know that I am literally a child of God. I am a part of his great plan and I have a purpose. I came from his presence and hopefully I will return to his presence. All good things come from our Heavenly Father. Good music comes from him and provides an extra dimension of communication. I consider it a privilege to bear my testimony through this extra dimension. I believe that Jesus is the Christ and the only begotten of the Father. I believe that he was crucified as a man and that he died for my sins. If I repent, I will be able to live with him again."

Realizing Your Dreams

1. "You have to have passion and really want to achieve your goal. There is no conflict with wanting to be the best at something and being an outstanding member of the Church. In fact, being a member of the Church should make you want to magnify your talents even more."

2. "You must be uncompromising in raising your personal standards and skill level. Being single-minded will keep your standards high."

3. "You need to have someone else who loves you and supports you to help you reach your goal. You cannot do it alone; you will need other people."

4. "Finally, you have to be willing to work. No matter how much passion you may have, if you are not willing to discipline yourself and put in the long hours, day after day, you will fall short of your desired goal."

The Powerful Influence of Music

"Music can have a great influence on our emotions. That is why it is so important to be selective about the music you listen to," said Ariel, shown in the illustration above with her daughter Neylan, a gifted pianist who often accompanied her mother during her career. "High-quality music, not only sacred music, can reach inside and lift you up spiritually. Conversely, listening to music with vulgar lyrics and rhythms that appeal to your baser instincts can wound your spirit. This kind of music makes you more susceptible to Satan's influence."

STEVE ANDERSEN

STEVE ANDERSEN was born in St. Anthony, Idaho, with a moderate to severe level of cerebral palsy. Cerebral palsy is any of several motor disorders resulting from damage to the central nervous system. Although walking and speaking have been difficult, Steve has never let his physical challenges prevent him from experiencing the fullness of life.

Reared on the family one-hundred-acre farm in Teton, Idaho, Steve developed a good work ethic. When he was three, his father began teaching him how to ride a horse. Staying on a horse was not easy for Steve, but riding helped him develop muscles and balance that enabled him to walk. He also learned how to accurately shoot his .22-caliber rifle. When he turned eight, he was sent to Boise to receive his education at a boarding school. Attending high school was one of the loneliest times in Steve's life. Fellow students regularly tripped him in the hallways and then laughed. "I remember being on my way to school when the kids on the bus set my coat on fire," Steve said. "They thought it was great fun."

On one occasion, he gathered the courage to sternly confront a member of the school's football team who had tripped him. "I told him that he hurt me when he tripped me in the hall," Steve said. "Once he learned that I had feelings too, I saw a newly found understanding come over his face. From then on, the harassment stopped and we actually became close friends."

Steve endured other challenges as well. One day while walking down the street, he was arrested and body searched. The way he walked and slurred his speech had led police to believe that he was intoxicated. Upon discovering their mistake, they apologized and promptly released him. Rather than making Steve feel sorry for himself, this incident and other difficult experiences have contributed to his desires to live a fulfilling life.

Steve furthered his education at Ricks College and Brigham Young University, where he earned a bachelor's degree in sociology and a master's degree in educational counseling. Being a college student also posed challenges, but fellow students assisted Steve with his reading and helped him to get across campus.

Steve's whole life has been about overcoming challenges and proving to people that although his way may not be the neatest or the quickest, he nevertheless can get the job done. As people learn of Steve's positive attitude and willingness to do his best, their attitude toward him changes.

People may think or say to Steve, "You can't do this or that," but his determination allows him to respond, "No, I *can* do this; let me show you."

Steve has always been an outdoorsman. Growing up near the Grand Tetons, he learned to love rock climbing, kayaking, snowmobiling, canoeing, downhill skiing, white-water rafting, hunting, and horseback riding. "Sometimes when he comes home from his adventure trips he will frequently be battered and bruised, but he is stronger inside for it," his wife, Shirley, said.

Rather than give up on difficult goals, Steve always tries to do his best so that he knows he made a worthy attempt. Scuba diving is a good example. For Steve, the ear pressure associated with underwater

Home on a Horse
Steve is at home anywhere as long as he's on a horse. "Horses are and will always be my first love," he said. Since the age of three, he has never let his cerebral palsy interfere with his horsing around. He rode his first horse by himself when he was nine.

Ascending the Mountain
The climbers are hiking through a mist of clouds at 16,000 feet. Steve, the second climber, holds on to metal tent poles for balance.

Mount Kilimanjaro
Mount Kilimanjaro, a giant stratovolcano composed of alternating layers of lava and ash, is believed to have erupted since the last ice age (within the past ten thousand years). Kilimanjaro is the largest of about twenty volcanoes near the southern end of the East African Rift Valley and is among the largest volcanoes on the earth. As all of Kilimanjaro's climbers know, the mountain's gentle lower slopes steepen to 30 degrees at about 13,000 feet.

activity is quite painful, but despite the pain, Steve experiences success in the trying.

As a faculty member of BYU-Idaho, Steve uses his love for adventure and the outdoors to bless the lives of others. He founded the Adaptive Service Adventure Program, which is designed to provide disabled students with active experiences they might not otherwise be able to have. Steve maintains his positive attitude by finding joy in accomplishing something new, and he encourages his disabled students to push their limits, try new things, and learn by experience what they can and cannot do.

In September 2001, with only two weeks of notice, Steve accepted an invitation to be a member of the first disabled climbing team to climb one of the most difficult routes up Mount Kilimanjaro in Tanzania. All who learned of Steve's goal to climb the rugged volcanic mountain were astounded, knowing such a feat would be difficult even without a disability.

The day following the September 11, 2001, terrorist attack on the United States, Steve and other members of the expedition arrived in Tanzania. Suspecting that they were potential fleeing terrorists, local authorities promptly arrested the group and threw them in jail. The mistake was soon rectified, however, and the group was released and allowed to continue its quest. Through the media, local Tanzanians learned of Steve's attempt to climb Kilimanjaro and began openly offering their support. They wished him well and expressed great admiration for him.

Steve's expedition traveled through jungle, desert, and volcanic terrain. One of the guides carried a loaded AK-47 assault rifle to protect the group from elephants, lions, or other predatory animals. During times of severe fatigue, Steve gained strength by humming the hymn, "O My Father." As the group approached the rim of Kilimanjaro's summit crater, Steve thought "about all the disabled people who dreamed of doing something extraordinary but were not given the chance to do so." Notwithstanding his own physical limitations, Steve felt truly blessed.

As the group neared the 19,336-foot summit, many were suffering from acute mountain sickness. The oxygen-thin altitude caused flu-like symptoms that, for Steve, resulted in muscle spasms that prevented him from walking and hindered his breathing. He was forced to stop just eight hundred vertical feet from the summit rim.

While descending the mountain and feeling defeated, Steve learned an important lesson. "Anyone who gives their all to something loves life and is to be respected," he realized. "Since I had given my all to climb the mountain, I was to be respected even though I had not completed it."

Despite his accomplishments in the face of overwhelming odds, Steve does not consider himself a hero. "I am just an ordinary guy doing extraordinary things, but by doing so I hope to help my fellow beings."

Downhill Action
A mono-ski allows skiers to glide downhill in a seated position. Mono-skiers maintain their balance using outriggers—forearm crutches that have small skis attached to the bottom. Most mono-skis have a feature that allows the seat to lift up in preparation for the ski lift. Steve uses a bi-ski, which is similar to a mono-ski but utilizes two skis for added stability.

Look Out Below!
In two jumps, Steve can drop about forty feet in three seconds. He teaches his students how to safely enjoy repelling.

Steve's Testimony
"If there is anything to learn from these experiences, it is to have faith in the Father of all. I really believe that he listens to our prayers and answers each one. He may not always answer the way we would like, but he is always there. I know that he is. I have experienced his spirit many times, and I have to believe that he has been watching over me. My life has been put on the line too many times while rock climbing, repelling, canoeing, kayaking, and horseback riding for me to believe otherwise. He is a preserving God who loves each of his children. His prophets walk the earth today, and if we but follow their counsel, we will be better for it. Jesus Christ died for us and is always there to assist us and give direction to our lives. I am grateful for the knowledge the gospel brings."

STEPHEN R. COVEY

STEPHEN R. COVEY filled his youth with activities ranging from marble tournaments to all forms of athletics. After winning nearly all the marble championships throughout the state of Utah, he competed in a national marble tournament in Denver, Colorado. With his steady hands and sharp eyesight, he took third place in the country.

When Stephen was not playing marbles, he was pursuing his intense love for sports. Pole-vaulting, swimming, soccer, and football occupied his time. His athletic days came to an end in junior high school, however, when his left leg collapsed under him while he was playing football. Doctors were perplexed to find that a disease was deteriorating his hip and thighbone.

"I will never forget hearing the doctors say I had to go on crutches for two weeks, and then they would look at it again, and how disappointed I was because I felt that was too long," Stephen recalled. Two weeks on crutches turned into six months, then a year. Eventually, doctors operated, inserting a nail. Impatient to be up and about following his operation, Stephen said, "I tried to start running again before I should have, and I had to go for another year on crutches. And then the disease spread to my right leg, and I had to have another nail put in that leg and go on crutches for a third year."

Stephen missed the thrill of athletic competition, but he didn't feel deprived because he began focusing his attention on academics. In place of sports, he developed a passion for learning, debate, and speaking. After receiving his undergraduate degree from the University of Utah, Stephen served a mission in England. Just a few months after his arrival there, he experienced a defining moment in his life when his mission president asked him to train branch and district presidencies throughout the British Isles.

The Temple—the Lord's University
"The temple has had an enormously significant impact on my life because I see it as the Lord's university, the perfect model home, and the greatest source of the deepest insights and learning ever vouchsafed to man," said Dr. Covey, who married his wife, Sandra, in the Salt Lake Temple on August 14, 1956. They have nine children and forty grandchildren.

Of that experience, he later said, "Even though I was a college graduate when I went on my mission, such a request was totally out of my comfort zone. I was a very young man training men two to three times my senior. I had no idea at all that I could train leaders. I was totally overwhelmed, but my mission president just said, 'You can do it.' That was significant. The experience was humbling, profound, and enormously soul stretching."

Stephen had found his niche in life, returning home from his mission with a growing sense of what would become his life's work. "I once told the grandson of my mission president: 'Your grandfather probably got me into this business of training leaders,'" he said. Following

Leadership and the Gospel
"First, realize that example is the highest form of leadership. In the last analysis, we teach what we are, not what we say or even what we do, even though what we are is closer to what we do. Only trustworthiness can produce trust.

"Second, we must become people of vision so that we see what is possible, not only in situations but also in people. In that way, they feel our communication to them of their worth and potential so clearly that they come to see it in themselves. We must also be people of great discipline governed by conscience, which is the spirit of Christ given to every person who comes into the world. Discipline brings vision into reality. When vision, discipline, and passion are governed by conscience, the world is lifted for good.

"The youth today must realize that they are a very, very special generation with a very special stewardship. I affirm to them their worth and potential, for it is way beyond the social definition. It comes from a divine source. Someone wrote, 'When man found the mirror, he began to lose his soul.' The point is, he became more concerned with his image than with himself. We must look into the divine mirror of the gospel, of the priesthood, of patriarchal blessings, and of the temple to continually deepen our understanding of our divinity and of our divine responsibilities so that we truly do see life as a mission, not as a career. We need to realize that it is not about me and mine but about thee and thine."

his mission, Stephen went directly to Harvard Business School for his master's degree and then completed his doctorate at Brigham Young University.

Whether working as a missionary, a university professor, or a corporate counselor, Stephen always considered himself more of a teacher than a speaker. He institutionalized his work and built an organization to support his teaching and speaking.

"My company grew little by little," he explained. "Because the content seemed to be helpful and uplifting to people, I was invited to participate in more and more speeches throughout the country and eventually throughout the world. I am a strong believer that the key is content, not technique; the key is character, not personality."

In 1997, Dr. Covey merged his corporate consulting and training programs with the Franklin Quest Company, a leading provider of training seminars and the creator of the Franklin Day Planner. The new entity, known as FranklinCovey Company, became the largest firm in the corporate training industry.

In addition to assisting the corporate world, Dr. Covey has sought opportunities to strengthen families and individuals. A month following the terrorist attacks in New York City, Dr. Covey hosted a free community workshop dedicated to strengthening family relationships. The event was created for families affected by the terrible events of September 11, 2001. The interactive forum offered an uplifting and encouraging environment to the community and to families who were forced to deal with unimaginable trauma.

World Leaders and Heroes

Dr. Covey has met with and counseled several heads of state, including presidents of the United States, South Korea, Mexico, and Uruguay. His experiences and associations with world and powerful corporate leaders have helped him form a personal definition of a hero. "Heroes to me are those who subordinate their ego to their conscience and dedicate their life to making a contribution. Heroes to me are those people, like President Gordon B. Hinckley, who never retire but who receive more and more of God's gifts and graces because they have been taken from those who neglect them and given to those who have magnified what they had earlier been given. A hero to me is a young person who stands true and stalwart in the face of great temptation and social pressure. A hero to me is one who is a transition figure in his or her own family, that is, in stopping the transmission of bad stuff from one generation to another."

Despite his celebrated national and international accomplishments, Dr. Covey remains firmly grounded in the gospel of Jesus Christ. "Without any question, the gospel has been the greatest source of strength to me during my career as an author and as a professional teacher and speaker," he said. "The gospel gives us an internal source of personal security so that we don't live for others' approval and so that our desire to please is subordinated to our desire to contribute."

Often, when teaching or speaking to large or important audiences, Dr. Covey said, "I find that reaffirming my sense of priesthood stewardship and realizing that I may be the only person they have heard with the priesthood give me almost an unbelievable sense of gratitude and power. Life is basically a mission and not a career, and since we are consecrated to building God's kingdom and establishing Zion in the world, everything else becomes a stewardship, including bodies, properties, and responsibilities."

Sharing the Gospel with Large Audiences

As a missionary, Stephen welcomed the challenge of introducing the gospel to and interacting with large groups of people. "During street meetings, I learned that the real key to getting larger audiences was to engage in some kind of respectful interaction with hecklers," he said. "Sometimes they were disrespectful, but I found that if I would keep my cool and treat them with respect and fairness, I would win over the majority of the audience, and they would become open and influenceable. About one-fourth of our baptisms came from such street meetings throughout Great Britain."

GIFFORD NIELSEN

GIFFORD NIELSEN learned at a young age the value of hard work and commitment—thanks to his parents' vision of involving their family in the lives of Brigham Young University students. Because Giff's family lived just above the university campus, his parents decided to start a program to prepare breakfast and dinner, Monday through Friday during the school year, for approximately thirty students.

By watching his parents and five older sisters prepare and sell meals, a project that helped the family make ends meet, Giff not only learned valuable lessons but also made new friends. Many of the BYU students who purchased meals became like older brothers, stopping by to play football, basketball, or baseball with Giff. So began his love of athletics.

Thanks to his father and grandfather, Giff also developed a love of the outdoors. Some of Giff's fondest memories include fishing with his grandfather, who joined the Church as a young man living in Denmark. Because of his deep convictions about the truthfulness of the gospel, he left his family and country to live among the Saints in America.

Reflecting on his grandfather's faith, Giff said, "I often think about what it would be like to say good-bye to my mom and dad to pursue a new life, having made a commitment to the Lord to embrace his gospel, knowing that perhaps I would never see them again. My grandfather was the pioneer who introduced the gospel to the generations following him. I talk to my children about the importance of knowing and honoring their heritage. Realizing that everything we do is building a legacy for future generations hopefully will give us strength to make righteous decisions."

While attending Provo High School, Giff displayed his athletic ability on the basketball court and the football field. During his senior year, his football team placed second in the state while his basketball team, following an undefeated season, won the state title. He entered Brigham Young University with scholarships in both basketball and football. After excelling in both sports for two years, Giff and his coaches decided that it was time for him to focus on just one sport.

Go by Faith

"I learned an important lesson when I was in college and had to choose between playing basketball or football. No matter what the situation, if you are saying your prayers and the Lord leads you in a certain direction, you go by faith. 'Trust in the Lord with all thine heart; and lean not unto thine own understanding' (Proverbs 3:5). If I would not have trusted the Lord, I would not have been a football player, broadcaster, or where I am today. No question, I cannot deny it."

"I put a lot of thought, effort, and prayer into that decision," he said. "I soon knew that I was supposed to play football."

Giff's career as quarterback for the Cougar football team began with several setbacks. Because he performed poorly in practice and during his first college start, he was demoted from starting quarterback to third string.

"For some reason I was unable to throw the ball well and complete passes," he said. "I was frustrated and as low as I ever could be. This was one of the first times in my life that I was really failing, and I could not seem to turn it around. Although my confidence was low, I never questioned myself because I had always been taught by my father just to 'do the best you can do and things will work out.'"

Giff's chance to redeem himself arrived during a game against New Mexico University. The Cougars were losing the game, and Coach LaVell Edwards sent Giff in with three minutes left in the third quarter. With help from the rest of the team, Giff immediately turned the game around with a series of touchdown passes.

"It was a magical evening. The crowd was going wild. We won the game, and the next day I was the starting quarterback," Giff said. "After the game I thought about how I had been failing in my athletic career. I had always been told not to give up. You never know what will happen; just don't give up!"

For three years, Giff led the Cougar football team to winning seasons and was BYU's first first-team All-America quarterback. When he was a senior, his team led the nation in scoring and total offense, and he was the leading candidate for the Heisman Trophy. With such a promising season underway, BYU traveled to Oregon to play Oregon State. After directing the team to a 14–0 lead, Giff was hit in his left knee and heard something pop.

"While caught up in the emotion of the game," he said, "I continued to play

with my left leg dangling beneath my left knee until finally I told the coach that I had to come out." His leg was wrapped on the sideline and examined carefully upon his arrival in Provo. The team's doctor informed him that he had to operate immediately because his medial collateral ligament had detached from the bone.

"One of the greatest moments of my entire life then happened," Giff said. "I looked into the faces of the athletic director, the trainer, the doctor, and Coach Edwards and knew that I could ask any one of them for a priesthood blessing prior to my surgery. Realizing that each of these great men was a worthy priesthood holder was very special to me. I knew right then and there that everything was going to be okay."

Although the surgery was a success, it ended Giff's college athletic career. Nevertheless, he was always upbeat about his circumstances.

The following year, Giff was drafted by the Houston Oilers. As a rookie in the National Football League, he worried about how he would fit in with his teammates while being faithful to his religious beliefs. After much prayer, he shared his values with fellow players. Most of them respected him for being true to his convictions.

"Sharing my beliefs with others prompted question after question about the Church," he said. "I even had a player approach me during NFL training camp about researching his genealogy. I learned a valuable lesson that day. If you stand up for your beliefs right from the start, even in the world of professional football where you have access to every vice known to man, being faithful will be much, much easier. In fact, my teammates eventually protected me. If they were going out to party they would say, 'Everyone is invited—except Giff.'"

After playing pro football for six years, Giff was approached by a Houston television station with the opportunity to become the station's sports director. After careful consideration, he accepted the offer even though he had no previous broadcasting training.

Giff and Wendy, his high school sweetheart whom he married in the Provo Utah Temple while attending BYU, have three sons and three daughters. Through his widespread and outstanding reputation, he was influential in winning public support for the Houston Texas Temple.

Success through Fundamentals

"My best years as a quarterback were when my skills were fundamentally sound. Before working on my throwing, my coaches would focus on my footwork, leg strength, and quickness. We worked on my quarterback drops, making sure that I knew where to be to make the plays. Then the mechanics of my throwing motion were rehearsed time after time. Mastering the fundamentals is crucial before working on other elements of the game. There are fundamentals in everything—in school, in football, in broadcasting, or in any other career. Focusing on the fundamentals in the Church and in your chosen profession will enable you to excel in life."

Success in Football and in the Community

"I have been so blessed in life, and I have always wanted to give back to the community. There are people out there struggling, and I want to serve them. In 1986, I started the Giff Nielsen Golf Tournament, benefiting more than 600,000 kids in the Houston area. A portion of the money raised is given to a board of directors consisting of forty high school students. As a board, they listen to the problems and issues of the community and then distribute the funds to the people they believe need it the most. An allotment of their funds goes toward building public parks in the Houston area. Kids without parks or swings or anything like that are now given a place to play. Serving others is very satisfying. What the scriptures teach about service is true. When you serve others, you feel better about yourself."

Sports Broadcasting

For nearly twenty years, Giff has worked for KHOU as sports director. In addition to broadcasting sports, he is responsible for the sports staff and the sporting news content. He assists in developing the station's sport shows, investigates news stories, and conducts interviews with local athletic stars.

SERVING AFTER 9/11

SEPTEMBER 11, 2001, was a day of shock and sorrow for all Americans—especially for those living in New York, Pennsylvania, and Washington, D.C. But with the sadness, loss, and scenes of disaster that accompanied the aftermath of that terrible day came countless acts of remarkable goodness and charity, numerous episodes of extraordinary humanity, and many examples of strangers helping strangers and people putting the needs of others above self.

"When we get in circumstances like this, there is only one true source of comfort—and that comes from God, our Eternal Father," said President Gordon B. Hinckley shortly after the attacks (Jason Swensen, "Pres. Hinckley on CNN," *Church News*, 22 September 2001, 5).

Following September 11, Americans turned to God as well as to each other. Members of The Church of Jesus Christ of Latter-day Saints were among the many who answered the call, giving comfort, offering service, and saying prayers. The Church donated financially to relief agencies, offered many chapels as a refuge to those in need of shelter, and planned memorial programs to show appropriate homage to the bereaved and injured.

The following stories are a small sampling of the Latter-day Saints who were willing to "mourn with those that mourn" and to "comfort those that stand in need of comfort" (Mosiah 18:9) by offering their time, resources, empathy, and, in some cases, homes.

Fields of Patriotism
The grounds outside many chapels around the country became fields of American flags. Some Church properties were adorned with more than one hundred flags.

Grueling and Dangerous Service
Just hours after the attacks on the World Trade Center, Shaun R. Parry signed up with the Red Cross as a volunteer. He was put to work near ground zero for four days—working twelve-hour shifts with only two hours of sleep between each shift. He performed numerous tasks, including directing volunteers, coordinating shelters, assisting at triage sites, and searching for survivors and bodies.

"I ended up working right on top of the World Trade Center itself, digging and pulling scraps of metal and whatnot," Shaun said. "I found a crevice, a big, long slab jutting sideways, jammed into the ground with all the beams still intact. On the south side I found a hole. Being a dancer and having gymnastics training, I was able to shimmy down the side of the beams. A whole cavern opened up behind it and [I could] follow it like a cave. I was able to shimmy down the side of beams and get about fifty feet below ground, looking for people." Volunteers who didn't know Shaun's name began calling him "Spiderman."

"Because I was the one down there, they sent camera and sound probes down, and I set [them] up to check for survivors, going in and out of the voids," he said.

Shaun needed silence in order to listen carefully for sounds of life, but digging shovels and machinery created a lot of noise. "It was so poignant when I was the one who was calling out, 'I need silence now,'" Shaun said. "They relayed it all the way out, and then there was absolute, dead silence. I called out . . . and waited in the pure silence to hear if anyone tapped back." Although Shaun didn't find any survivors, other rescuers located eleven in the first two days after the towers came down.

"You would not believe the cheer that went up when they would say, 'Yes! We found someone!' Everyone just cheered. That's what we were there for. Everyone was screaming, 'We got one! We got one!' It was amazing—the power of love and open hearts" (John L. Hart, "Moments of Heroism Found in Grueling Service," *Church News*, 22 September 2001, 9).

Wall-to-Wall Beds

Two hours before it was to land in New York City, Delta Flight 149 from Europe dropped suddenly from thirty thousand feet to twenty thousand feet and made a sharp right turn. The captain told the plane's passengers that they had been diverted from New York City, and he promised an explanation once they had landed. "Ladies and gentlemen, it is difficult to tell you what I have to say," he said once the plane was on the ground. "Please remain calm. The United States has been attacked."

The passengers listened with tears in their eyes as the captain shared details of the day's attacks. For security reasons, the passengers deplaned with nothing but the clothes on their backs. In a few hours, nearly five thousand airline passengers had been diverted to St. John, Newfoundland.

Members of the St. John Branch immediately volunteered their time and their small building. The chapel was soon filled with two hundred makeshift beds, and the kitchen was filled with soup and sandwiches. Additional food and supplies had to be stored in cars because every nook in the chapel was full. People slept wall-to-wall in the classrooms, offices, and hallways, and branch members and missionaries worked around the clock, serving donated food and shuttling stranded travelers to stores and medical offices.

"Some wonderful and enduring friendships were formed during this trying time," said Sharna Redinger, branch Relief Society president. "There was not a time in those six days when activity stopped, and the Spirit never left. All the things we had learned in the callings we had held throughout our Church lives came into practice then. Organization, cooperation, patience, prayer, and listening and relying on the Holy Ghost were needed. We truly had the opportunity to bear one another's burdens. We mourned with those that mourned, we tried to comfort those who stood in need of comfort, and we stood as witnesses of God."

The strangers who landed on their doorstep became strangers no more, Sharna added. "'Those' passengers became 'our' passengers, our friends, and, finally, our brothers and sisters, which they had been all along."

Falling Debris the Size of Cars

Jonathan Hill emerged from the subway beneath the World Trade Center about five minutes before nine o'clock the morning of September 11, 2001. As he walked toward an exit, he overheard several people talking about a disaster at the World Trade Center. Still trying to make his way to work, Jonathan soon found himself staring in unbelief at the northwest tower, where smoke and flame were leaping from high-story windows.

"As I walked north of the World Trade Center, I heard more gasps and a sound like thunder," Jonathan recalled. "I turned around to see an enormous explosion lower on the other tower. The explosion etched an image in my mind that I will never forget. Almost immediately after the blast, I saw pieces of glass, metal, and other debris, some the size of cars, raining down on the street where I stood, so I ran for cover into a shoeshine store at 109 Church Street."

Just as he ran into the store, Jonathan said, "I looked behind me and saw that a man about two steps behind me was hit in the head by falling debris." At the risk of his own life, but deciding that he had no choice, Jonathan quickly exited the store to pull the injured man to safety.

After helping the man into the store, Jonathan and the storeowner used shoeshine rags to stem bleeding from a six-inch gash the man had suffered. Then they quickly called 911. As additional victims rushed into the store, Jonathan administered first aid and gave comfort to as many victims as he could. He then willingly stayed at the store until emergency personnel arrived to evacuate the victims.

A Quilt Becomes a Healing Memorial

More than twenty women contributed their time and talents to create a memorial quilt honoring firefighters who fell at the World Trade Center. Many of those women were members of the New York, New York Stake Relief Society; others were neighbors eager to take part in a worthy cause.

The quilt's genesis came from fireman John Eccleson (Ladder 79, Engine 22, Staten Island), who was seeking an artistic way to commemorate the losses of the New York Fire Department (FDNY). He wanted the artwork to feature the names of all the firefighters who lost their lives.

To include all firefighter names, the quilt was made from approximately fifty squares. The prepared squares were then distributed to the women, who embroidered seven names on each square. The quilt also featured emblems of the FDNY and four lines of the "Fireman's Prayer":

> AND IF, ACCORDING TO MY FATE,
>
> I AM TO LOSE MY LIFE.
>
> PLEASE BLESS WITH YOUR PROTECTING HAND
>
> MY CHILDREN AND MY WIFE.

The women, some of whom learned to embroider specifically for the project, worked on the quilt amidst the smells of smoke and dust and the realization that their city would never be the same. But serving the fallen firefighters helped them deal with the tragedy and find healing.

On June 15, 2002, firemen at the Staten Island firehouse gratefully accepted the quilt. Captain Frank Hudec expressed heartfelt appreciation for their handmade gift, which he noted had required much loving work and attention. Today, the quilt is on display at a fire department on Staten Island.

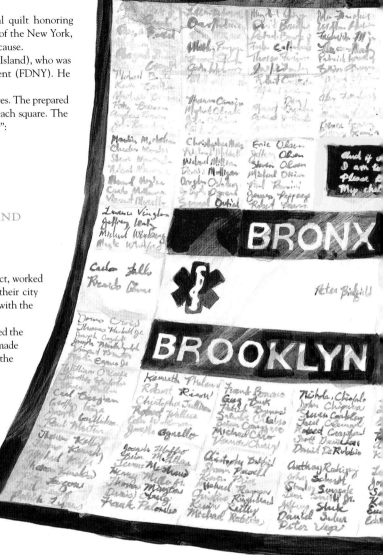

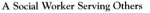

A Social Worker Serving Others

Serving and assisting children is one way Kristy Stone contributes to her community. As a social worker in East Harlem for the past three years, she works with families in crisis who are dealing with some form of abuse or neglect. She is amazed by people's strength as they struggle day-to-day to overcome painful challenges. Kristy has devoted her life to helping others because she believes that people "are good at the core and have much potential."

On September 11, Kristy refocused her skills and training on those who had lost loved ones. She was a friend to those who needed a friend and a blessing to many in time of need. "I listened to their stories—story after story," she said. "I held their hands. I tried to be strong for them."

Kristy believes that the gospel plays a role in emotional and physical recovery because it gives a bigger perspective. "It comforts and heals and renews faith," she said. "Just knowing the whole plan of happiness allows us to put tragedy into perspective and be comforted, knowing there is a higher plan and that Heavenly Father ultimately is in charge."

350 Blankets Comfort Victims

Several months before September 11, Relief Society sisters in the Victorville California Stake began making homemade security blankets to be donated to Project Linus, a charitable organization that gives blankets to children affected by trauma. When a call went out for blankets a few days after the terrorist attacks, the sisters were ready. Their 350 blankets went to St. Vincent's Hospital in New York City, where staff distributed them to children who were injured or who lost parents in the attacks ("350 Blankets Comfort Victims," *Church News*, 27 October 2001, 14).

Bake Sale Brings
$851 for Attack Victims

Wanting to contribute in some way to relief efforts, Elizabeth Tew decided to travel to New York City so she could dig through rubble to help find survivors. But because she was only ten years old, her parents encouraged her to devise another plan. So Elizabeth and a few of her friends decided to hold a bake sale and donate the proceeds to the American Red Cross Disaster Relief Fund.

Within days after the attacks, a team of youthful volunteers from the Pottsville Pennsylvania Branch, including Elizabeth, Brett New, Chelsea New, Claire Harlos, and Sierra Bodner, had organized the first September 11 fund-raiser in their area. The bake sale included a tempting display of lemon bars, marble brownies, Texas sheet cake, chocolate chip cookies, cherry-topped vanilla cake, fresh loaves of bread, and two kinds of soup—all donated by corporate sponsors and individuals from the community.

Eager for an opportunity to support the relief effort, people flocked to the bake sale, which was held in a shopping mall. Although Pottsville is not an affluent area, patrons made generous contributions, including an elderly lady who gave a hundred dollars. Others offered to buy a dollar's worth of cookies for ten dollars. With assistance from parents and Primary leaders, the young people raised $851. A local corporation then matched the bake sale proceeds, doubling the amount donated to the relief fund.

Providing Cool Water to Firefighters

On the day after the terrorist attacks, Kris Wooley, Kyle DeMordaunt, and three others noticed people unloading cartons of bottled water from a boat on the Hudson River. Realizing that the workers were shorthanded, the five volunteered to help. Kris and Kyle, former missionaries, soon found themselves delivering cool water to grateful firemen who were rummaging through the World Trade Center rubble.

When the water supplies ran out, Kris and his friend Mike Coleman, also a returned missionary, drove a van a mile north to acquire more donated supplies. They ended up working until 3 A.M., filling cups with ice, water, and other beverages, and wading through soot and burned-out buildings to bring relief to emergency personnel.

"They were so appreciative," said Kyle. "Feelings were somber, and they had more on their minds than thanking those who offered a cool drink, but they expressed their appreciation" (Shaun D. Stahle, "A Tragedy Reverberates around the World," *Church News,* 22 September 2001, 8).

Chad Hawkins, Jacob Hawkins, and Dale Murphy

CHAD S. HAWKINS, author and illustrator of the best-selling book *The First 100 Temples*, graduated from Weber State University with a degree in fine arts. His unique artwork, which often includes hidden images, has appeared in the *Ensign* and *New Era*, is on permanent display in the Vernal Utah Temple, is included in the cornerstones of several temples, and is found in numerous private collections throughout the United States.

Chad, also the author of *Youth and the Temple*, is a popular speaker at youth firesides, devotionals, conferences, and Especially for Youth camps. In illustrations throughout *Latter-day Heroes*, Chad has hidden the names of his wife, Stephanie, and their children—Jacob, Anne, and Rachel. Chad and his family reside in Layton, Utah.